Let The Blessed Say "Amen"

A Word from the Lord

Thirty - One Days of Encouragement and Testimonies

George M Guy

DEDICATION

CONTENTS

FOREWORD

Day 1

Untitled

May 27, 2020

Please trust this, and believe this word from the Lord.

The Lord is night unto them that are of a broken heart; and delivereth them out of ALL of their troubles.
Psalms 34:18

The two key words here are nigh and all.

Nigh – close to, within reach, about to happen

All – total, everything, nothing left

The two major things that this scripture is addressing is a broken heart and troubles.

Sad to say, but most of my Facebook friends are suffering from one or both these things in their lives.

There is no quick fix for a broken heart. The healing is a process. We must allow God to heal our broken hearts.

Healing takes time, but the way you survive until your broken heart is healed is believing that God is nigh.

Saints of God, if you have Jesus close to you, it brings a comfort and an assurance that you're going to make it.

Then God's word says that He will deliver us out of all of our troubles. That could represent family problems, financial woes, job troubles, health problems, or anything else that is bothering you today.

Every child of God needs to tell the devil today, "I'm trusting and believing today that Psalms 34:18 will be fulfilled in my life. God is going to heal my broken heart and deliver me out of all of my troubles."

This is the day to confirm the Word by shouting "Amen, I believe!"

From His precious Word to bring comfort to His children,

G. Guy

Day 2

Kindness

May 25, 2020

This is a long post, but everyone needs to read this.

Webster says that kindness means warm hearted, considerate, humane, sympathetic, showing consideration.

And be Ye kind one to another, tenderhearted, forgiving one another, even as God for Christ's sake hath forgiven you.
Ephesians 4:32

In my observation of life and people, I've found that kindness is a natural instinct to people that have the spirit of God in their lives.

I didn't say all that claims to be religious. If you claim to be a child of God and not have a kind spirit, your religion is in vain.

But the fruit of the spirit is love, joy, peace, longsuffering, gentleness, goodness, faith. **Galatians 5:22**

Without any of these, you are lost. Kindness is a direct result of these 7 fruits of the spirit.

My precious, old, and Godly grandfather used to say, "When you turn a bucket over, what's inside is coming out." What he was saying was if you cuss, have anger issues, rudeness, and wrath in your heart, it's going to come out.

On the other hand, if kindness is in your heart, it will show. It's as natural as breathing.

When I react wrong to people, and I have before, I make sure to apologize quickly, and find me an altar and repent. When my heart is pure, kindness is reinstated.

I'm not bragging or gloating over having this attribute in my life, but yesterday in Market Basket, our local grocery store, I was in line checking out behind 2 young girls. Both of them were between 10-12 years old. They had $6 and a gallon of milk in their hands.

I stepped up to the cashier and said, "I'm going to pay for their milk with my purchase." I then told the girls to tell their mother, "An old man wanted to bless us." I told them that they could have the $6 and that God loves them.

This small kindness gesture caused a reaction from several people. The lady checking out ahead of the girls was deeply moved. She said what an act of deeply moved. She said what an act of kindness that was and asked my name and what I did for a living.

I witnessed to her and told her about my Facebook daily postings. She stopped me outside and wrote my name down where she could ask to be my friend.

I looked up and one of the little girls said to me that her mother wanted to talk to me. I walked over to the vehicle, and she let the passenger window down and thanked me for my act of kindness. She tried to hand me the $6 back, and I told her to not steal my blessing, and that was just a love letter from God telling her that He loved her. It moved her deeply.

I looked on the console and saw a pack of cigarettes. I then said to her, "I'm going to pray that God helps you to quit smoking. This is why God put this together." I told her about my ministry and Facebook posts and gave her my name.

What a day that was. It all began with just a small act of kindness. Another one of my Pawpaw's sayings was "Son, you will catch

more flies with honey than with vinegar."
My grandfather was the example of
kindness. To be Christ like is kindness.

It's time to take inventory. Are you kind to
your family, your friends, your companion,
and your co-workers? What about your
waitresses and even people that are rude?
That is no excuse. Jesus was kind to those
who treated him poorly.

*A soft answer turneth away wrath, but grievous
words stir up anger.*
Proverbs 15:1

A soft answer is being gentle and kind.

I try every day to show kindness to all I
meet. Start today and see the effect that
kindness will have in your life.

If you are an old grouch, why don't you get
ahold of yourself? You are going to have a
lonely life if you don't. Nobody will want to
be around a rude, grouchy, loud person.

Somebody shout, "Amen". This is a matter of Heaven or Hell.

This is from the word of the Lord.

G. Guy

Day 3

Untitled

May 24, 2020

Just some solid rock preaching that will keep you blessed and saved.

For your soul's sake, read this.

A word fitly spoken is like apples of gold in pictures of silver.
Proverbs 25:11

If you don't have anything good to say, it's best to say nothing at all. With our tongue, we have the power to kill or make alive.

Whoso keepeth his mouth and his tongue keepeth his soul from troubles.
Proverbs 21:23

It won't happen every time, but it's a good sign if you're having a lot of trouble that you probably can't control your tongue.

Go ahead, speak your mind, say what you think, and say hurtful things. It hurts us deeply just to speak out against another, but remember this, the hurting is not over. Your days and life will be full of troubles, of self-inflicted wounds if you continue.

I know all of you are thinking of someone who needs this post. Before you decide to send it to someone else, make sure you are not guilty. It's so easy to see a mote in your brother's eye when there is a beam in your eye according to Matthew 7:3-5.

Keep thy tongue from evil, and thy lips from speaking guile.
Psalms 34:13

But the tongue can no man tame; it is an unruly evil, full of deadly poison.
James 3:8

I have to fight this every day. We all must learn to bridle our tongues, or we will be lost.

I said, I will take heed to my ways, that I sin not with my tongue: I will keep my mouth with a bridle, while the wicked is before me.
Psalms 39:1

If any man among you seem to be religious, and bridleth not his tongue, but deceiveth his own heart, that man's religion is in vain.
James 1:26

I worry about people that know the latest gossip on people that have fallen into sin.

Today, let's watch everything we say. Let's let our words be those of healing, of encouraging, of lifting up. Do this, and watch your life change, and your day be filled with blessings and not trouble.

I remember a story that my grandpa told me. He said there was a man in the community that never had anything to say about anyone. Nothing but good things came out of his mouth.

There was another man that was a devil – full of hate, wouldn't provide for his family, stayed in jail, abused his wife and children, and he hated everyone.

He died, and some men decided that they were going to try to get the good mane to finally say something bad about someone. They went over to the good man's house and asked him if he had heard about the evil man's passing. The good man informed them that he had heard about it. The meddling men asked the good man what he had to say about it. The good man paused for a while and then, with a smile, said, "He sure could whistle good."

Please, this day and every day, try to find the good in everybody, and if they can't even whistle good, just say nothing at all.

These are things I have to watch in my life. I'm not throwing stones, but I'm just trying to help you get to Heaven.

Someone shout "Amen" or "Help me, Lord".

From His Word,

G. Guy

Day 4

Correction, Direction, Protection

May 24, 2020

Three things that you must allow the word of God to do for you.

All scripture is given by inspiration of God, and is profitable for doctrine, for reproof, for correction, for instruction in righteousness:
2 Timothy 3:16

1. Correction

Son of man, I have made thee a watchman unto the house of Israel: therefore hear the word at my mouth and give them warning.
Ezekiel 3:17

God has placed a preacher in your life to bring you the word from the Lord to keep you saved. We must receive correction from His word to keep us saved.

2. Direction

There is a way that seemeth right unto a man, but the end thereof are the ways of death.
Proverbs 14:12

Enter ye in at the straight gate: for wide is the gate, and broad is the way, that leadeth to destruction and many there be which go in thereof:
Matthew 7:13

We must depend on the word of God to put us on the right road that leads us to everlasting life.

3. Protection

A thousand shall fall at thy right side, and ten thousand at thy right hand; but it shall not come nigh thee.
Psalms 91:7

For he shall give his angels charge over thee, to keep thee in all thy ways.
Psalms 91:11

You that have given their lives to Him do not have to fear anything that comes against you. God has sent angels to protect you in everything that comes against your life.

Every one of you need to say today, "Lord, correct me, direct me, and protect me." Can the church say, "Amen"?

Something from His word that will help you make it to your eternal home.

G. Guy

Day 5

The Desperate Need of a Daysman

May 24, 2020

Neither is there any daysman betwinxt us, that might lay his hand upon both of us.
Job 9:33

Daysman – An arbitrator, one who stands between two parties and tries to bring them together, to settle an argument, an umpire

In the book of Job, it tells us that he desired someone to put one hand on God's shoulder and one hand on his shoulder and reason them together.

A daysman in simple terms means a peacemaker.

The devil has tried his best to turn mothers against fathers, fathers against mother, children against parents, and parents against children. His desire is to completely destroy the values of a happy family.

The precious memories of Sunday dinners at MaMa and PaPa's house, with all the family gathered together in precious love and unity, are some of my favorites. Hearing PaPa Holland bless the food and pray for God to keep us together and serve him with all our hearts was so mobbing. They are some of my most precious childhood memories.

With the way things are today, it breaks my heart. It is with great embarrassment to tell you that we have had holidays with part of our family not there because of some cross words or falling out between some of our children and grandchildren.

Nothing breaks the heart any more than to see your family divided. I'll never give up. I am determined to be a daysman. Thank God at this moment, we are all together.

Father, mother, son, and daughter, there has got to be some give in all of us. The hardest thing you will ever do is take the humble side. You win with God when you do this. If any of you know of division anywhere, let God use you to be a peacemaker.

I don't want to be known as a divider, or one who makes matters worse between people. I want to be a peacemaker.

Blessed are the peacemakers; for they shall be called the children of God.
Matthew 5:9

I pray for all of you that have your families divided. I pray that somebody would let God us you to be a daysman, a peacemaker, and heal everything that has separated you. Let's all have some give in us to accomplish this.

We could all meet, and not discuss the problem or argue about who's right or wrong, but to have an old time family prayer meeting. Then get up, hug one another's necks, and say three words, I love you. Imagine how blessed we would be.

Your reward for this is you will be called a child of God.

Follow peace with all men, and holiness, without which no man shall see the Lord.
Hebrews 12:14

That's pretty plain. We must seek to be at peace with all men to see God.

This is a hard post. God moved on me with a heavy burden to bring churches, families, marriages, and friends together, or we will be lost regardless of who is at fault.

In closing, there's an old saying, "We must bury the hatchet." Don't leave the handle out. Put things under the blood so God won't be ashamed to be called our God.

Blessed are the peacemakers.

I don't know why I'm saying this, but somebody better listen. Don't wait until you get to the graveyard and live in regrets because you didn't heed this warning. Let today be a new beginning in your life.

This word from the Lord needs to be shared with all your friends. If you believe this, at least say "Amen".

Directly from the heart of God

G. Guy

Day 6

Things You Get When Your Ways Please the Lord

May 23, 2020

When a man's ways please the Lord, he maketh even his enemies to be at peace with him.
Proverbs 16:7

I have made up my mind that I want to please the Lord. I want to please Him in all my ways. I must please him in the way I act, the conversations I have, the way I treat my neighbors and loved ones. I must please him in my church attendance, prayer life, and my daily actions.

By doing this, God will even make my enemies be at peace with me.

I would ask all of my readers to find out what pleases the Lord and what displeases

Him. Do everything in your power to please the Lord every day.

If you fail, you must repent and start over. Don't quit, just wipe the dust of failure off, and love Him with all of your heart.

Someone say with me today, "I am going to please the Lord." Do this, and watch your life change when you accomplish this.

From His word,

G. Guy

P. S.

I thought I might go ahead and mention a few things that displease Him.

- Jealousy, Envy
- Hate, Strife
- Grudges, Bitterness
- Unrepented sins
- Being offended and/or offensive
- Unfaithfulness to church
- Gossip

Day 7

God Really Hears Your Prayers

May 21, 2020

O thou that hearest prayer, unto thee shall all
flesh come.
Psalms 64:2

We must believe God's word that tells us He hears every prayer that we pray. Sometimes when I pray, it feels like my prayers didn't even reach the ceiling of the room where I knelt to pray, but that is not true.

God hears every prayer that is prayed from a sincere heart. God answers prayer.

Prayer will remove fear. Elisha's servant at Dothan saw the enemy surrounding the city, and fear gripped his heart. Elisha prayed, and God opened his eyes to see the true picture.

That prayer removed fear because God opened the servant's eyes, and he saw a host of angels around about them. Prayer will allow you to see the answer instead of the problem.

Prayer makes God bigger than the devil or the mountain you face. Prayer-less people are powerless people.

I feel led of God to pray for all of you that have fears and need miracles in your life today.

Lord Jesus, I humbly come before you. I want to say, first of all, how much I love you. Thank you for loving me and answering my prayers. Today, my precious, Heavenly Father, I ask you to open the eyes of all my friends, and let them see the power of prayer and what it can produce. Remove fear, doubt, and guilt for every heart that reads this. Let them know that you love them and that you are a prayer answering God. In JESUS name I pray today. Amen.

Now, you must rise in faith and believe that God has heard our prayers. Go ahead and shout, "I am going to pray more." Somebody shout, "I believe in prayer."

This is your answer from His word.

G. Guy

Day 8

You Must Believe That God is About to Show Up in Your Storm

May 21, 2020

Back in 1972, we lived out of Vidalia in the country off Airport Road. That night, around midnight, a horrible thunderstorm came. Just before this, I had made up my mind that our 4 year old son, Richy, was not going to sleep with us anymore.

He cried about it, but he was in the bed with his older brother, George. All of a sudden, the lightning lit up the sky, and the thunder was awful. The lights went out, the rain beat down, and the wind was blowing strong.

I looked up to see Richy, at the foot of my bed, shaking and horrified. He was crying, begging to sleep with us. I said loudly, "No, go back to your room."

After a while, I heard him sobbing at the door. My sweet wife said, "Honey, I know you've told him he can't sleep with us, but let me make him a pallet beside you on the floor."

I was already looking for a way out of my decision; so I agreed. He laid down right beside me on the floor when the loudest crash of thunder hit. The sky lit up, and then, it went totally dark.

Shaking and crying, he said with a shaky voice, "Daddy, do you love me?" I replied, "Richard, you know I love you." He said, "Daddy, if you loved me, you wouldn't want me down here by myself all night."

I had already told him that he couldn't come where I was; so I climbed out of my bed and went to where he was. I wrapped my arms around my little boy on the pallet and held him until all the fears were gone.

There are times, in all of our lives, that darkness covers us. There are problems on every side, and we feel so alone. We wish, sometimes, we could leave here and go to where God is. That's not possible, but I can assure you that God will come to where you are.

For he has said, I will never leave thee, nor forsake   thee.
Hebrews 13:5

That's a promise we can depend on. I pray each of you would believe this word from the Lord, and let Him calm your fears today.

Just like I loved my boy, you must believe that your Heavenly Father loves you.

Somebody make the devil mad, and shout, "Amen"!

Just a love letter from Your father to You,

G. Guy

Day 9

The Power of Prayer

May 20, 2020

But ye, beloved, building up yourselves on your most holy faith, praying in the Holy Ghost. **Jude 1:20**

This scripture tells me that there is a way to build me up or strengthen me. It also tells us that it will increase our faith.

The answer, in 5 words, is "praying in the Holy Ghost". It takes 2 things to accomplish this.

- Prayer
- The Holy Ghost

If you have Jesus Christ alive in your soul and are living a righteous life, every time you pray you are praying in the Holy Ghost.

We are powerless without prayer. Prayer changed you from ordinary to extraordinary. Prayer controls 3 worlds. It controls:

- Heaven
- Earth
- Hell

My purpose for this post is to stir all of my friends to get involved in prayer. Prayer will heal disease and sickness. Prayer will bring prodigals home, put marriages back together, and provide financial needs in your life.

If there is true prayer, there is no worry. If there is no worry, there is no prayer.

There are times when you pray and feel nothing, but don't quit. God is hearing and recording your prayers.

Sometimes it's good to put on some soft gospel music when you pray. When I pray, I ask God for the needs I have in my life.

While I am asking God to keep a hedge of protection around me, around my family, around my friends and loved ones, I'm giving my praise to Him for all He has done for me. I'm also saying these words, "I love you, Jesus."

Pray without ceasing.
1 Thessalonians 5:17

Prayer must become a habit, an addiction.

It is my burden and prayer today that, all of you reading this, would realize your need for more prayer. I will continue this study on prayer tomorrow.

Am I helping anyone? Somebody that sees this and needs this shout, "Amen"! Make a commitment to God today to pray more.

This is from the word of the Lord.

G. Guy

Day 10

Let God Use You

May 21, 2020

Someone you know today desperately needs you to encourage them at this moment.

The liberal soul shall be made fat: and he that watereth shall be watered also himself. **Proverbs 11:25**

What this means is when you bless someone, God is going to abundantly bless you. When you encourage someone, and God will see to it that someone encourages you.

What I felt in my heart today is the desperate need of encouragers.

Battles, trials, troubles, disappointments, broken dreams, depression, family troubles, and worries leave us wondering if we are going to make it and if anyone even cares.

In valleys, sometimes all it takes is a phone call or a message to help someone make it through a bad day.

I pray every day for God to lay someone on my heart that needs a word of encouragement. That's why I write this daily posts.

Why don't we let God lay someone on our hearts today? Make a phone call, send a text, or send a letter, and let them know that you care and are praying for them.

I'd like some of you to tell us about someone that has encouraged you in a short post. It may be all someone needs today is a simple phone call with these words, "I had you on my mind, and I'm praying for you. I love you."

What a needed ministry in ALL of our churches?!

I've got some encouraging words from the Lord to you today. You're going to make it. His amazing grace is sufficient. He still loves you in spite of your past failures. Hold on, the storm is about to pass.

Directly from the word of the Lord...and oh yes, I love each of you, and today, I ask God to bless you.

From His word,

G. Guy

Day 11

What Goes Around, Comes Around

May 19, 2020

Kindness produces kindness. Bitterness produces bitterness.

Therefore all things whatsoever ye would that men should do to you, do ye even so unto them; for this is the law and the prophets. **Matthew 7:12**

Man, if you are thinking about a scripture that will turn your life around, this is it. I have done my best to live by this principle every day that I live.

Very seldom do I encounter anyone that's rude to me. I'm going to show respect to everyone I meet each day, and most of the time, I receive the same respect that I give them.

I tip everywhere I go, and I love to tip in advance. I usually tip at least 20%, but most of the time, I tip more. Even if I'm at McDonalds, I give them a tip.

I'm going to be nice to the clerks at the gas station because I may be the only example of Jesus Christ that they will ever see. It has happened before, but not very often that after I treat them good, they were rude to me.

Before you react wrong, you need to consider that they may have been abused, or their heart may have been broken that day.

I'm going to take the high road and return good for evil. You win with God when you do that. To be Christ like means to act like Christ. We must manifest this spirit in our everyday living to please the Lord.

Let's all watch our attitudes, our manners, and the way we respond to people. This may save someone and lead them to Christ.

I'm always looking for a way to get your response to my post. Your input is very important to me. I pray every day and ask God to let me help someone that needs an answer from Him.

Let the church shout, "Amen"!

This will help you have a happier life.

From His word,

G. Guy

Day 12

Sometimes, You've Just Got to Press On

May 19, 2020

I press on toward the mark for the prize of the high calling of God in Christ Jesus.
Philippians 3:14

The greatest thing that has ever happened to us is being filled with His Holy Spirit.

That qualifies us to a heavenly home not made with hands. A land of no more sorrow, tears, pain, or death. What a great prize that can be obtained at the end of this race.

There are hills, valleys, trials, and powers of hell that will try to stop us on our journey home. God never promised us a life of ease, but He did tell us that His grace would be sufficient to see us through all of our problems.

The word "press" means to just keep moving forward, to push steadily, to follow through, or to force forward.

I'm serving notice to the gates of hell. I've caught a glimpse of my prize and felt the power of the high calling of Jesus, and I am going to press every day.

I have fought a good fight, I have finished my course, I have kept the faith: Henceforth there is laid up for me a crown of righteousness, which the lord, the righteous judge, shall give me at thy day: and nor only to my only, but unto all of them also that love his appearing.
2 Timothy 4:7 – 8

Paul had to press.

Can I get you to commit? I'm not giving up. I'm pressing forward. Let those that have overcome say, "Amen".

This word is for the ones that realize that you have a prize waiting for you, Jesus.

G. Guy

P. S.

It's going to be worth it all.

Day 13

Let Us Go Into the House of the Lord

May 19, 2020

I was glad when they said unto me, Let us go into the house of the Lord.
Psalms 122:1

Our attitude about going to church today will determine what we get in the house of God.

I was with Bro. Billy Cole in Ethiopia years ago about 20 miles from the crusade site when we saw people coming off a mountain dancing and praising God. There were over 200 of them. I asked Bro. Tecklemarian what they were doing. He said, "We believe in Psalms 122:1. We believe if you're glad going to church, when you get there, God will answer your prayers."

That day, 11 blind eyes were opened, there were lame being healed, and many other miracles took place. Why don't we try that today?

Enter this gates (church) with thanksgiving, and into his courts with praise; be thankful unto him, and bless his name. **Psalms 100:4**

Let's try this today, and report a miracle. He awaits your praise.

G. Guy

Day 14

Comforting Words

May 19, 2020

The Lord thy God in the midst of thee is mighty; he will save, he will rejoice over thee with joy; he will rest in his love, he will joy over me with singing.
Zephaniah 3:17

The 3 revelations that God wants you to see in this post are:

1. You're not by yourself, God is in the midst of thee
2. He is not going to let you down. He is going to save you.
3. You can be at rest because he really loves you.

These are comforting truths that will make you a lot happier if you will believe the word of God.

When problems arise and the enemy comes against me, I tell the devil, "I'm not by myself. God is with me. Greater is He that is within me." That greater is Jesus.

The word says He is mighty. Did you hear that devil? My God is mighty, greater than any problem, bigger than any mountain, and He loves me.

You're not going to torment or trouble me any longer. He is my God, and He loves me. He is going to take care of my needs. I'm going to sing unto the Lord, a song of victory.

Now I must ask all of my Facebook friends this question. Do you believe the word of the Lord, or do you believe the enemy (the devil) that has been tormenting you?

Somebody shout, "I believe the word of the Lord. He will save me."

From His word,

G. Guy

Day 15

A Word from the Lord – God Has Heard Your Prayers

May 19, 2020

Then he said he unto me, Fear not, Daniel: for from the first day that thou didst set thine heart to understand, and to chasten thyself before thy God, THY WORDS WERE HEARD, and I am come for thy words.
Daniel 10:12

Daniel, an anointed man of God for that day, felt a burden to seek the Lord for answers, and He had a desire to have the power to be able to withstand the demonic spirits that were coming against the people of God.

For 21 days, he set his heart to seek the Lord with prayer and fasting. He felt that he was getting nowhere, but he held on. On the 21st day, he had a breakthrough. The angel appeared to him and said, "God heard your prayers the first day, but the demonic powers of hell has tried to stop me from getting here. God sent Michael, one of the chief angels to help me bind the devil."

Here is what God sent me here to tell you.

And said, O man greatly beloved, fear not, peace be unto thee, be strong, yea be strong. And when he had spoken unto me, I was strengthened, and said, let my Lord speak; for thou hast strengthened me.
Daniel 11:19

What is so wonderful about this story is, first, he was strengthened, and he also received an answer on how to achieve victory in future problems.

My word for you today is: Hold on, don't be discouraged, keep praying, God has heard your prayers.

The devil has tried to hold things up that you are praying about, but you are about to have a breakthrough. This is what God spoke to my heart for you today.

God sent Michael to help the angel fight the Prince of Persia, God will anoint you to bind the devil that is holding up your answer.

I'm praying now. Keep praying with me.

It would be a good time to say, "Thank you Jesus for hearing my prayers." Let the believers say, "Amen".

Yours in His service,

George Guy

P. S. I really feel a mighty breakthrough. Hold on.

Day 16

No Power, No Miracles

May 19, 2020

Now unto him that is able to do exceedingly abundantly above all that we ask or think, according to the power that worketh in us. **Ephesians 3:20**

If we could all believe this one scripture and qualify ourselves to receive these promises from God's word, our lives would be so much happier.

Do you really believe that God can do above what you have the power to think in your minds?

The children of Israel, going to the promise land, would have been very happy with houses they didn't build, wells they didn't dig, and vineyards they didn't plant.

What a blessing it was to get these things, but watch what God gave them, things above what they thought they were getting: cattle, gold, silver, treasures, servants. He proved he is a God of abundant blessings.

Now the rules for qualification: ACCORDING TO THE POWER THAT WORKETH IN US.

What is the power that works in us?

That power is produced by prayer, faithfulness to church, dedication, reading God's word, fasting, treating others right, living above sin, singing the songs of Zion, and worshipping God with all of our heart.

Everything we do toward God faithfully produces power that results in miracles. This is the only way to get the power of God to work in your life. No short cuts. Just old time dedication and living right every day.

Today, why don't we all purpose in our hearts to do everything in our power to get God's power working in our lives?

Let the church shout, "Amen"! We are not waiting on God. He is waiting on us.

This is right out of the word of God to help us obtain miracles in our life.

G. Guy

Day 17

Watch Your Reactions When God Punishes Your Enemies

May 16, 2020

Rejoice not when thine enemy falleth and let not thine heart be glad when he stumbleth: **Proverbs 24:17**

This is a powerful word from the Lord that will keep you from making a tragic mistake.

We have all known people that have done us wrong. When we allow God to fight our battles, they will eventually suffer for the wrong that was done to us as children of God. (God's word declares it.)

When judgment day from the Lord comes for them, what will be your reaction?

Now, you will have to be really careful how you act on that day.

Although they are suffering because of their actions, because of how they hurt you, or because of how they did something against you, you will have to watch your reaction. If you rejoice or make statements similar to "That's what they get", or "They deserve the pain that they're experiencing now," God will be angry at you. It angers Him when you rejoice over your enemy falling or being punished.

Watch your attitude, or God will reverse the curse. It would be the same as you, a parent, correcting your children. It breaks your heart to punish them in any way, but because of your love for them and for them to turn out right, it must be done.

You would become angry if your other children made statements about the child being corrected. Your love for the child that has done wrong never changes. God feels the same way about His children that have to be corrected.

This is why you have to be so careful how you react when God punishes your enemies. It could cost you a lot of sorrow.

Some need to say, "Help me Lord." Can the church say, "Amen"?

From His precious word to help you be saved,

G. Guy

P. S.

It doesn't mean he hates you when he corrects you. He just wants you to repent and start over.

Day 18

The Promise and The Premise

May 16, 2020

All of you need to read this strong word from the Lord.

All scripture is given by inspiration of God, and is profitable for doctrine, for reproof, for correction, for instruction in righteousness. **2 Timothy 3:16**

I have been posting a message daily on Facebook since 2013. In every message I post I have seen if it's something from the Lord, I'm positive my readers and comments double.

If it's a message of instruction or warning, the readers are very low.

What we all must realize is to every promise in the word of God, there are qualifications to receive the promise.

It's called THE PROMISE and THE PREMISE.

The PROMISE is the blessing we get, and the PREMISE is what we have to do to get the PROMISE.

There are so many today that all they want to hear is the positive, and they never want to hear the requirements. Please be careful that you don't fall into that category.

It is the ministry's duty to encourage you, but it is also their responsibility to reprove and correct you by God's word.

This is just a warning from the Lord to some of my precious Facebook friends that need to change your thinking about messages of warning or correction from the Lord.

I hope I haven't lost my following. I'm still trying to get you saved and blessed.

Can I get one "Amen"?

Yours in His service,

George Guy

Day 19

A Strong Word from the Lord

May 15, 2020

In prayer for you today, God spoke this to my heart. Your season is about to change.

And let us not be weary in well doing: for in due season we shall reap, if we faint not. **Galatians 6:9**

Weary – worn out in strength and energy; having one's patience and pleasure exhausted

Due season – at the right time; in a short time

Reap – to harvest; the rewards for labor being done

Faint – to like strength; to become weak; lose courage

I come to you today with a strong word from the Lord. Hold your head up high, and be encouraged in the Lord that your season is about to change.

Every seed you have planted is about to break through to a great harvest and reaping.

I remember as a child that my precious grandfather, Rev. W. W. Holland, would let me help him plant a garden. I thought that we would never see the evidence of life beneath the soil.

After the rain and sunshine, and what seemed to me a long time, we walked out one morning and saw the breaking in the crust of the soil from the seed that we had planted.

There was a new hope and joy that came into my heart. We had the evidence that reaping in due season was about to happen.

I felt in the spirit that your winter time is about over. You have endured the trying of your faith. The sun is about to come up. You are going to see the evidence of new life.

Be encouraged in the Lord, and keep the faith. It's time to see some great changes for the better in your life.

We pray for you every day.

Yours in His service,

George Guy

Day 20

Faith That Produces Miracles

May 14, 2020

Your faith can never produce a miracle until it's put in a place where it is challenged.

Daughter, be of good comfort, they faith has made thee whole.
Matthew 9:22

This woman had an issue of blood, had spent all of her money, and was in a place of no hope. She heard about Jesus and pressed through the crowd to touch the hem of his garment.

She had said to herself, "If I may but touch His garment, I shall be whole."

It's great to have a miracle, but it took the suffering of an issue of blood to produce one. You can never have a testimony of Him calming the storm in your life until you are in a storm.

What I feel God has for us today is this: don't despair if you have a need or an impossibility in your life.

It is time to tell yourself that He is about to give me a miracle. I have faith in Him. I shall have a testimony.

His first words to this lady were, "Daughter, be of good comfort." (Free from fear)

Her faith in Him made her whole. She left with her miracle. Say with me today, "He's my father. My faith is in Him. I shall have my miracle today."

Still trying to get you blessed.

From His word,

G. Guy

Day 21

So You Made a Mistake, Start Over

May 14, 2020

For all have sinned, and come short of the glory of   God;
Romans 3:23

This is the antidote.

Verse 24 goes on to say: *"Being justified freely by his grace through the redemption that is in Christ Jesus."*

Justified – to provide a good reason for the actions of someone

Grace – mercy, forgiveness, kindness, unmerited favor

Redemption – buying back, the act of saving people from sin and evil

This statement may bring you comfort, "The only people that have never made a mistake are self-righteous people that in their eyes are perfect."

So you messed up, join the crowd. We all have sinned and come short of the rules of God. Forgiveness and mercy are just a repentance away.

Hiding your sins, justifying your shortcomings, and blaming others will cause you to be lost. Some of you are too embarrassed to go back to church and are worried about what others think of you.

True children of God are thrilled that you are back, and they will never question you about your failures. It is only the self-righteous hypocrites that don't want you back.

Let today be a new beginning for many of you. You've already asked God to forgive you. Don't doubt the power of His blood. Get back up, wipe the dust of failure off of you, and start over. Forgive yourself, and watch God bring back the new.

Somebody shout with me, "By His grace, I will be saved." Everybody should say, "Amen".

This will keep you saved.

G. Guy

Day 22

I'd Rather Have Jesus

May 12, 2020

There is an old familiar song that has been on my mind for the last few days. How many of you remember this old song?

I'd rather have Jesus that silver or gold
I'd rather have Jesus than riches untold
I'd rather have Jesus than houses and land
I'd rather be led by His nail pierced hand

Those old songs still move me. There are so many people that say this, but the bottom line is they trade Him away for the least of things.

Let me mention a few things that people choose over Jesus: a moment's pleasure, alcohol, drugs, tobacco, adultery, cheating, a night on the town, bitterness, grudges, hatred, lust, things of the world

No man can serve two masters: for either he will hate the one, and love the other: or else he will hold to the one, and despise the other. Ye cannot serve God and mammon.
Matthew 6:24

Many say with their lips, "I'd rather have Jesus", but yet they choose some of these things that I have listed.

Don't tell me how much you love Jesus if you still offend those around you. Don't say you love Jesus, but you still smoke, drink, curse, lust, and hate your neighbor.

Before you give in to sin, think about what you will have to forfeit. You may have to pay for the rest of your life and all of eternity for the choices you make.

I wish somebody would lift your hands and say, "I'd rather have Jesus." Can the blessed say, "Amen"?

A solid word from the Lord to help us make the right choices.

G. Guy

P. S.

We had no idea that Sis. Vonnie Lopez was going to sing this song at his funeral. She had another song chosen, until the night before the service. She messaged us to ask if she could change at the last minute, and now it's obvious as to why she felt to sing this one. No other song could've embodied our Poppa more than this one. He not only loved this song, but he lived it. Jesus before anything.

Day 23

The Power of Love

May 10, 2020

Let brotherly love continue.
Hebrews 13:1

My little children, let us not love in word, neither in tongue; but in deed and in truth.
1 John 3:18

He that loveth not knoweth not God; for God is love.
1 John 4:8

A new commandment I give unto you, That ye love one another; as I have loved you, that ye also love one another By this shall all men know that ye are my disciples, if ye have love one to another.
John 13:34 – 35

I feel that so many people are going to be lost because of bitterness, grudges, and hate toward people that have done them wrong. We must get over these things, or we will be eternally lost.

It may not have been your fault, or they may have never apologized to you. They will suffer for this, but if you allow it to make you bitter, you have a great problem.

I don't have to elaborate on this. Just read my scriptures, and find out how God feels about love. John 13 tells us that we are to love one another as much as God loves us.

When we fail to do this, we cut off the blessings in our lives. Love isn't the words you say with your tongue. It is deeds and actions that prove your love.

To let the world know that we are His disciples is not done by how much you pray, how holy you dress, or what church you attend. It is done by how much you love one another.

"By this shall all men know that ye are my disciples, if ye have love one to another."

This post is meant to wake us all up, and make us realize that it's the littles foxes that spoil the vine.

To let me know that I'm not wasting my time, someone say with me, "Help me Lord." Can I get just one "Amen"?

This is still in the Book.

G. Guy

P. S.

This does not mean that you have to hand out with them or have them back in your trust, but our heart must be right toward them. No hate or grudges.

Check your heart today.

Day 24

More of Him, Is That Your Heart's Desire?

May 14, 2020

As the heart (deer) panteth after the water brooks, so panteth my soul after thee, O God. **Psalms 42:1**

O taste and see that the Lord is good: blessed is the man that trusteth in him. **Psalms 34:8**

My soul longeth, yea, even fainteth for the courts of the Lord: my heart and my flesh crieth out for the living God. **Psalms 84:2**

Once you have received the gift of the Holy Ghost and experienced the power, protection, deep peace, and that feeling you feel of being in the Master's hands, there is nothing that can satisfy you like that feeling.

What is so sad is that many of you have allowed stress, failure, or just pressures of life, to remove you from that special place.

You've tried to fill that void with things of this world, but I'm here to tell you that there is nothing that can satisfy your soul like Jesus can.

What it took in the beginning to bring this joy in your life will still work. We must go back to what God first fell in love with – a clean heart that loves everybody, a right spirit, and a heart that cries out for more of Him.

I'm telling all of you that He is calling you today. He desires to put His arms around you now and calm every storm in your life.

Draw nigh to God, and he will draw nigh to you. **James 4:8**

You can accomplish that with prayer and reading His word.

Somebody needs to shout to the Lord this moment, "I'm drawing closer to you." Let the hungry say, "Amen".

This is a love letter from the Lord to all of us.

G. Guy

Day 25

Never Place a Period Where God Has Placed a Comma

May 8, 2020

This post is just for those that desperately need a word from the Lord.

A period means it's over – end of sentence, nothing else, conclusion of the matter.

A comma means there's more to the story – something else to be said.

When the enemy comes in like a flood,
Isaiah 59:19

Did you see that? It's not over, COMMA. I'm not giving up, God's not through. Before I have a breakdown, I'm going to read the rest of the story.

Here is the rest of the story.

The spirit of the Lord shall lift up a standard against him.

Now it's time for the period. Every time this will happen. God has the last say.

Here's why some of you are so stressed out. The enemy has told you....

Your family will never be saved. Period You're going under financially. Period

You must have cancer. Period Nobody loves you. Period You will never be happy. Period You will never be used of God. Period Period. Period. Period.

...that the enemy is coming in like a flood, and the Bible says he will come in like a flood; but some of you have allowed him in your life to put a period where God has placed a comma.

Now let's read it God's way instead of the devil's way.

My family is lost, Comma BUT God is going to save them. Period

I'm in a season of financial trouble, Comma BUT God has never failed me. Period

Weeping may endure for a night, Comma BUT joy comes in the morning. Period

Sometimes a rebuke is in order. I'm telling you in Jesus' name to quit accepting the devil's period, and have faith in God. The story is NOT over.

Somebody needs to say, "Oh me," and repent. Can I hear an "Amen"?

Please accept this word from God and rejoice in the Lord.

Why don't you be brave enough today or tomorrow to speak your testimony? Post what you think God is about to do.

This is a word from the Lord.

G. Guy

Day 26

From Sackcloth to an Ephod

May 8, 2020

Thou hast turned for me my mourning into dancing: thou hast put off my sackcloth, and girded me with gladness. **Psalms 30:11**

Mourning represents sadness, and dancing represents happiness and joy. It is not the will of God for His people to live in mourning every day. We will have times of sorrow, but we can't have this as a lifestyle.

When people, in biblical days, had a need or sickness in their lives, they would put on sackcloth. This was a rough, burlap type of material.

Also, in biblical days, the priest would wear a garment called an ephod. This was a praise garment. It was like a coat that was draped over their shoulder.

You can never wear sackcloth and an ephod at the same time. If you have the ephod on, it gets rid of the sackcloth. If you have sackcloth on, it gets rid of the ephod.

When I have sorrows and problems in my life, I put on the ephod, I praise God, and it always produces gladness.

There was a law – no sackcloth beyond the King's gate. To have access to our King today, we must put off our sadness and enter into His gate with thanksgiving.

It's your choice today. Live in mourning every day of your life, or live in dancing and gladness.

Where are the believers today? Somebody say with me, "My mourning is going to change to gladness. I'm getting rid of all my sackcloth, and I'm finding my ephod."

This is God's will for your life.

G. Guy

Day 27

The Rewards of Living in Hope

May 7, 2020

A special message that will help you.

H – Having

O – Only

P – Positive

E – Expectation

Thou art my hiding place and my shield; I hope in thy word.
Psalms 119:14

Hope – to want something to happen or be true, to truly believe it will happen, to expect with confidence

Hope is an ingredient that we all must have in our lives. Without it, we are all most miserable. My interpretation of hope if having only positive expectation.

My mind is made up. No negative attitudes, no negative doubt, and no negative statements. I'm holding on to every promise in His precious book.

For we are saved by hope:
Romans 8:24

Happy is the man that hath the God of Jacob for his help, whose hope is in the Lord his God.
Psalms 146:5

If you have lost your hope, you have lost your faith. Without faith, it is impossible to please God. This next scripture will tell some of you why you have lost your hope.

It is good that a man should both hope and quietly wait for the salvation of the Lord.
Lamentations 3:26

There are two things required in this scripture:

1. Hope
2. Quietly wait

The salvation of the Lord is the answer to what you have been waiting for. It's time for all of us to HOPE without wavering, having no doubt, and holding on until the answer comes.

Somebody shout with me, "I'm getting my hope back." Can the church say, "Amen"?

This is from the word of the Lord to save and help us.

G. Guy

Day 28

How to Determine Your Path

May 6, 2020

Path – a route you choose in life

In all thy ways acknowledge him, and he shall direct thy path.
Proverbs 3:6

Acknowledge – recognize

What this scripture is saying is to put God first in every part of our lives. Honor Him on the job, and when you get blessed, you recognize that God did that for me.

I put Him first in all my plans, business affairs, travels, buying things, problems, and victories. When you make Him a part of your life, He has a promise to direct your path.

No wonder David said, "Yea though I walk through the valley of the shadow of death, I will fear no evil."

How can David say that? He would say, "I have acknowledged the Lord in all my ways, and He has directed my path. Why should I fear?"

I pray over everything I do every day. This assures me of a great and blessed day.

Can I get a witness? Somebody shout, "Amen! He has directed my path. I'm having a great day."

This is the word of the Lord.

G. Guy

P. S.

There are times we put our desires and what feels good to us first. That path is very costly and very painful.

Pray this prayer, "God, not my will, but thy will be done." Acknowledge Him.

Day 29

Please Don't Live in Regret

May 6, 2020

No pain is any worse than when you fail to do this.

Train up a child in the way he should go and when he is old, he will not depart from it. **Proverbs 22:6**

This is not a suggestion from the Lord but a command. Look at what the word of God says about being saved, and teach them every day the principles of living for God.

As a young man, I took flying lessons to fly an airplane. My instructor, my trainer knew what it took to fly a plane. He never varied from the manual but followed it to the letter.

When the word says train them up in the way you'd have them go, you must understand that you are basing your options and rules on the Bible.

Some of you are going to live in regret if you allow your children to have their way. For example, when it gets to church time, it's not their decision as to whether they go or stay home. It is your choice.

None of us have been perfect in raising our children, but now that they are grown, you must put your trust in God.

They may not be living right at the moment, but I'm believing God's word that they are doing to die right. They will not depart from the faith.

This will bring comfort to you today. Start speaking faith, and believe God's word that your children are coming back to God.

Somebody shout, "I believe the word"! Some may say, "Help me Lord".

From His word,

G. Guy

P. S.

Parents, watch what they watch, keep a close eye on their cell phone, watch who they hang around, and watch how they dress. You must set down some rules, and tell them, "You won't smoke or drink as long as you are in my house." You are not training them right if you don't abide by this.

Day 30

The Danger of a Maelstrom

May 5, 2020

You will never forget this story.

Maelstrom – cyclone in water, result of conflicting tides, powerful currents

It could be 3 miles across the top and over a mile deep, like a funnel in water.

Off the shores of Norway, many years ago because of the rock formation and strong tides, a maelstrom would form every few days.

Three brothers fished that bay. It yielded great catches. In a large boat with nets full of fish, one day, they were carried so far away with their catch that they stayed too long. The maelstrom had formed already.

With a downward pull, they began to circle that formation gradually moving toward the bottom.

Hell from beneath is moved for thee...
Isaiah 14:9

One of the brothers fell in the water to his death. Another panicked and grabbed a hold of the anchor on the front of the boat and froze in terror.

The other realized the empty barrels that were slung off would float to the top. He tied a net around a barrel and tried to pull his brother loose and save him. He, in terror, would not let go.

Finally, at the last moment, he ran to the net and barrel and cut it free. He pushed it overboard and held on for his life. It floated him out, but he said the worst thing was hearing his brother's screams as he reached the bottom.

Life, problems, habits, lifestyles will put us all on this downward pull. Hell is determined to destroy us all.

I've come with good news – Jesus is the answer.

Some of you may hold on too long. I beg you to let go, take Jesus by the hand, let Him change you, and pull you from the pits of hell and baptize you with His power.

I'm a living testimony that He can set you free from that downward pull. Let the delivered shout "Amen"! Someone commit, "I'm going to be set free."

From His word with a warning,

G. Guy

Day 31

The Power of Impartation

May 8, 2020

For I long to see you, that I may impart unto you some spiritual gift, to the end ye may be established;
Romans 1:11

One of the greatest accomplishments that I have ever had in my life is when I gave up my church that I pastored for 22 years and submitted my life to the late, great Pastor Murrell Ewing.

He later introduced me to the greatest harvester and crusader that has ever lived, Bro. Billy Cole. He took me under his care and taught me how to be a harvester.

I was so blessed when he spoke words of impartation over me and my wife. That night, at his bedside, I felt his anointing come on me.

I have preached crusades all over the world. Every time I preach, I can feel the mantles of Bro. Cole on me. As long as I'm alive, Bro. Cole will never die.

I have reached the age of 72 now, and I have realized that I must impart my gifting to others. I have a team, Restoration Ministries, that works as close to me as I worked with Bro. Cole.

I have trained them to have crusades, Billy Cole style, and now many of them are ready to lead their own teams. They have a great harvest. As long as these men are alive, I will never die.

It is my desire, my prayer that God will add years to me and my precious wife's lives to see the fruits of our impartation.

If any of you would like to be a part of that ministry, let me know. It's not a one man show, it's a team effort. If you are a saint, you must have your Pastor's consent.

Prayer warriors, singers, musicians, evangelists, teachers, prophets, pastors, apostles, and harvesters are very much needed to shake this world with revival.

Please keep us in your prayers. We intend to finish this race with a great harvest.

Yours in His service,

George & Sybil Guy

WORDS FROM THE FAMILY

It's amazing to me that in today's society of social media and social distancing that family values can still maintain a value. I was blessed to have, what I considered, the greatest man of God be not only my preacher, but so very lucky to have the honor of calling him, "my daddy". He had a unique gift when speaking to me so that even when I knew I had done something wrong to upset him, I also knew that he did forgive me and that he would always love me. Now, there isn't a day that goes by that his guidance doesn't follow me. Maybe it's something he had told me before, but I am just now beginning to understand. One of my favorite things he used to tell me when I was struggling was that the right choice in everything isn't always the easiest. If you say you can't do something, then just maybe you didn't try hard enough. Just say that you can't hardly do it, and one of the most important parts was, "Son, the road to hell isn't a bad, dark, scary road. That's why so many people walk it. It's smooth, and it seems easy to travel on because the devil doesn't want you to know that you're on the wrong path." I didn't understand this at the time, but after his death, I started feeling like God turned his back on my family by taking my dad. It did seem so much easier to walk the other way, it wasn't a hard talk, my feet didn't hurt, and at times, it was even very peaceful. It wasn't until I was reading an old Bible of his, and not because it was the Bible, but because it had his handwriting in it that it hit me what Dad had meant. In that moment, I realized my faults for doubting God's decision and asked for forgiveness because the truth is the devil doesn't bother people that's heading in the direction he needs them to travel. It's when you turn and try to walk the right way that it always seems to get hard, life tends to be a struggle, but it's simply because you're headed in the right direction, and if the devil makes that walk almost bearable to walk with constant obstacles that it begins to feel like the wrong direction. I learned from my daddy that forgiveness isn't for those who ask for it, but it's for yourself to let go and move forward. He would truly forgive them, then turn around and fix a plate for them. He would say, "You came empty, but you left full." He loved everyone equally. He loved a sinner and prayed for them just as much as he would pray for a preacher friend of his. I hope in the years to come that there are times I can make him look down, smile, and say, "That's my boy."

Nicky Guy

AN UNSUNG HERO

There are a few things that my dad has done over the years that I would like to mention.

He pastored a great church, Faith Tabernacle, in Vidalia, LA, for 22 years. Four different times, I have watched as he gave cars to evangelists or saints that had no transportation. The bags of groceries, utility bills paid, rent payments made, and money given to those in need are far too many to try to mention. Let's not even start with the number of young people that he moved into our house and raised as his own.

Bro. Billy Cole got to the point in life where he was needing a caretaker and help making his house wheelchair accessible. My dad took him and Sis. Cole on two bus trips to minister in different churches, and those trips resulted in him raising around $149,000.00.

When Puerto Rico was destroyed by a hurricane, God spoke to him that he must become the widow and the raven for the pastors there. With the help of Daren Snider, Clark Rone, Bro. Tim Cooper, and Bro. Terry Ballard, he was able to two trips and place $1,000 into the hands of each of the 25 ministers and $2,000 into the hands of each of the missionaries there. Many were dying from bad water. With the help of Clark Rone and Bro. Tim Cooper, he was able to also send over 100 water purifiers.

Prior to Bro. Ewing's passing, God spoke to him with a way for our church family, Eastwood Pentecostal Church, to pay off Bro. Ewing's house. Within a year, we say that come to pass.

He went with Bro. Cole to Ethiopia on several trips and went four times with his own team. He has led crusades in the Caribbean six times. When he pastored his church, he helped build two churches in Old Mexico. Over the years, he has been there over 40 times preaching crusades with Bro. Scott Guinn. He worked under Bro. Billy Hale with the A team to Kenya and had traveled there 10 times. He was still doing crusades with his team, Restoration Ministries, in the Philippines just months before his passing. He had 28 major crusades there and saw thousands receive the Holy Ghost. During the COVID pandemic, he raised around $10,000 to feed different churches and saints there.

With his great faith and anointed gifting, he has helped pay off several churches in the UPC.

He and my precious mother, Sybil Guy, at 72 years old were still continuing to evangelize around the world, even in the midst of the pandemic. Both of them had health issues, and both of them continued to sacrifice for the kingdom.

Since 2013, even while hospitalized with COVID, he had posted daily messages of hope, faith, correction, doctrine, and encouragement on Facebook. Thousands of followers read them every day.

I just thought some of you maybe didn't know the sacrifices that my parents have made for the kingdom. They have given money, health, and their lives to ministry for over 50 years.

Thank you for allowing me to bring to you some of the accomplishments of my dad and mom, George & Sybil Guy.

Shronda Guy Miller

P. S. I forgot to mention the thousands of gold dollar coins that he bought with his own money over the years. He was still giving them out as a symbol of faith to let people know that God was going to help them and their family.

Made in the USA
Columbia, SC
23 August 2022

65268692R00065